D1443255

Mysterious Encounters

ALIENS

Peggy J. Parks

KIDHAVEN PRESS

An imprint of Thomson Gale, a part of The Thomson Corporation

THOMSON

———————★ ™

GALE

Detroit • New York • San Francisco • New Haven, Conn. • Waterville, Maine • London

Picture Credits:

Cover photo: © Royalty-Free/CORBIS; © Bettmann/CORBIS, 10 (main photo), 19, 37, 40; Raymond Fowler, 17; Hulton Archive/Getty Images, 26; Mary Evans Picture Library/Michael Buhler, 36; Burton McNeely/Time Life Pictures/Getty Images, 12; © Dale O'Dell/Alamy, 10 (inset), 24, 41; © Dale O'Dell/CORBIS, 5; Paramount/The Kobal Collection, 15; Victor Habbick Visions/Photo Researchers, Inc., 6; © Michael Waine/CORBIS, 28; Williams Archive, 33.

© 2007 Thomson Gale, a part of The Thomson Corporation.

Thomson and Star Logo are trademarks and Gale and KidHaven Press are registered trademarks used herein under license.

For more information, contact
KidHaven Press
27500 Drake Rd.
Farmington Hills, MI 48331-3535
Or you can visit our Internet site at http://www.gale.com

LIBRARY OF CONGRESS CATALOGING-IN-PUBLICATION DATA

Parks, Peggy J., 1951–
Aliens / by Peggy J. Parks.
  p. cm.—(Mysterious encounters)
Includes bibliographical references and index.
ISBN-13: 978-0-7377-3518-5 (hard cover : alk. paper)
ISBN-10: 0-7377-3518-X (hard cover : alk. paper)
1. Human-alien encounters—Juvenile literature. 2. Unidentified flying objects—Juvenile literature. I. Title.
BF2050.P37 2007
001.942—dc22
                                                                2006025574

38563010   10/08

Printed in the United States of America

Contents

Chapter 1

THE UNEXPLAINED

Since ancient times people throughout the world have claimed that they saw aliens and **UFO**s (unidentified flying objects). Some of them tell of encounters that occurred on Earth, or while flying in the air. Others say they were taken away on alien spacecraft to strange, unknown lands. The experiences these people describe range from wonderful and exciting to terrifying. Some even view their encounters as enlightening because they gained knowledge they did not have before. As different as their stories are, though, one common thread ties them together: They will never forget what happened to them.

Since ancient times, people all over the world have claimed to have seen aliens.

Gumby Creatures

One person who claims to have encountered aliens is an artist named John Velez. He says he has been face-to-face with the creatures on more than one occasion. According to Velez, his first encounter occurred in 1978. He saw a huge, formless light moving across the sky. At first he had no idea what the object was.

Aliens are often described as having large eyes shaped like almonds.

He later remembered that it looked like some sort of spacecraft: a silver metallic object shaped like a disk. It had a bright red light rotating on the top and a green light on the bottom. On other occasions, Velez saw different types of UFOs. One was shaped like a huge, black triangle, and another was just a big round orange blob of light.

Velez claims that all of these UFOs were spacecraft that carried alien beings to Earth—and the creatures were like nothing he had ever seen before. In the first group, the aliens had pear-shaped heads, pointy chins, and large black eyes. Velez says their bodies were very thin, with "arms like Gumbies . . . rubbery things."[1] In a later encounter, Velez says the aliens had dark bluish or purplish skin and were dressed in robes of rough fabric similar to burlap.

Velez says that when he saw the aliens, they communicated with him. Some of them had the power to see into the future, and they told him Earth was doomed. When they gave Velez a glimpse of their vision, he saw a very grim picture. He was shown how humans were harming the planet through pollution and other destructive practices. He also saw that because of human carelessness, the world would eventually be destroyed by "floods, fires, disasters of every imaginable kind."[2]

Tall, Short, Bald, Hairy

Velez's story is just one of thousands. Many other people claim to have seen aliens as well. Even if they were not given visions of the future, their encounters were still memorable.

Aliens have been described in many different ways. Some of the creatures were said to have huge, glowing eyes, while others had no eyes at all. People tell of aliens with tiny crinkled ears or floppy ears as big as an elephant's. There have been reports of aliens covered with hair, and others with no hair at all. Some people recall aliens that had faces but no noses and mouths.

A Massachusetts woman named Betty Andreasson reported multiple encounters with aliens. Some of the creatures had huge eyes attached to stalks that protruded from headless necks. Others had pear-shaped heads with slits for ears, noses, and mouths. Their eyes were large and catlike and wrapped around their heads.

The one feature that people often agree on is the height of aliens. They are usually described as being much shorter than humans. According to Velez, for instance, the aliens he encountered were only about 3 feet (1m) tall. The creatures in the second group were even shorter. But even though aliens are most often described as small, that is not always the case. An Italian security guard named Fortunato Zanfretta said he was abducted in 1978 by monsterlike aliens that were 10 feet (3m) tall. He said they had green skin and yellow triangles for eyes. Their ears were pointy, and their heads were covered with red veins.

"It Was Like Seeing a Ghost"

Just as people have described aliens differently, they also give varied descriptions of their spacecraft. In most encounters witnesses say they saw a UFO before seeing any creatures. These UFOs have been described as shiny, saucerlike disks, or cigar-shaped objects. Some people say they heard the craft whirring loudly as they raced through the sky. Others recall enormous balls of blinding light that hovered soundlessly above the ground.

New York resident Monique O'Driscoll reported seeing a UFO in 1983. She was driving home when she saw something astounding in the sky. It was a dark gray mass that resembled an enormous wing and was covered with brilliantly colored lights. O'Driscoll watched in disbelief as red, white, blue, and yellow lights flashed up and down the strange

This photo, believed by some to show a UFO, resembles an artist's drawing (inset).

spacecraft. The lights were so bright that she had to shield her eyes. Still she could not bring herself to turn away. She continued watching for about ten minutes, as she explains: "I looked up and was dazzled by the lights. . . . [They] were flashing like crazy. . . . Then the object made a slow, tight turn as if turning on a wheel and drifted slowly toward the east just over the trees. Then it was gone. It just vanished."[3]

O'Driscoll was not the only witness to the strange blinking spacecraft. Ten or more people who lived nearby saw the same thing. They described a boomerang-shaped object with colorful blinking lights that silently glided over their homes. Then about three weeks after those sightings, more reports of the UFO began pouring in. Hundreds of frightened people called the police to tell what they had seen. Their descriptions of the spacecraft were eerily similar to the accounts of others who had seen it.

The Hudson Valley Mystery

The November 1984 issue of *Discover* magazine claimed that the Hudson Valley sightings were all part of a major spoof. In an article entitled *UFO Mystery: Explaining the Hudson Valley Sightings*, the UFOs were said to be a group of small planes flying in formation. The "Stormville Flyers," as the magazine called them, had allegedly outfitted their planes with multicolored flashing lights and flown together at night to fool people.

These Hudson Valley sightings, as they were known, continued for about a month. By the end of March, several thousand people had reportedly witnessed the same object. One of them, a woman named Ruth Holtsman, expressed the shock she felt when she saw it: "It just hung there motionless in the sky," she said. "It was like seeing a ghost."[4]

A man points to what he claims is the footprint of an alien.

Were They Dreaming?

Holtsman and others who claim they have encountered aliens have a hard time telling their stories because people do not believe them. Even though thousands of witnesses have reported such encounters, people usually think they made the stories up. That is partly because so many alien accounts have proven to be hoaxes. Also, it is difficult for people to believe in something they have not seen with their own eyes—especially when it involves such a strange occurrence.

There are, however, many respectable people who claim they have seen aliens. Scientists have reported encounters, as have military officials, police officers, pilots, business professionals, and astronauts. These people realize their stories sound far-fetched. They knew they would likely be ridiculed for reporting what they saw. Yet many of them have refused to remain silent about their experience. They hope the time will come when nonbelievers find out how wrong they are. Jim Marrs, author of the book *Alien Agenda*, explains this point of view: "Only those persons whose outlook prevents them from dealing honestly with the massive amount of [evidence] still cling to the idea that nothing soars in the skies of Earth but man's imagination. . . . Of course, arguments . . . will continue. There are, after all, some few folks who still refuse to believe that the world is round."[5]

Chapter 2

MYSTERIOUS JOURNEYS

Jim Marrs bases his beliefs about aliens on what he considers to be solid evidence. He is a well-known author and researcher who has been investigating such stories for years. Marrs has learned about many different types of alien encounters. Some of them involved people who willingly took journeys with alien beings. Others involved **abductions**, or situations where people were forcibly taken to unknown locations.

The Strange Blue-Green Light

One alien abduction reportedly occurred in November 1975. An Arizona man named Travis Walton was driving home from work along with some coworkers.

Suddenly the men noticed a large glowing disk hovering above a clearing in the forest. Walton jumped out of the truck and ran toward the craft. As the others watched in shock, the craft shot a blue-green ray of light at Walton and knocked him unconscious. His friends were so terrified that they drove away. Later they returned to the scene, but they found no trace of Walton or the UFO.

Walton reappeared five days later on a road about 12 miles (19km) from the abduction site. He

D.B. Sweeney (right) played alien abductee Travis Walton in the 1993 movie *Fire in the Sky*.

told of a strange and frightening encounter with aliens. After he had been knocked out by the beam of light, he regained consciousness in the spacecraft. Three aliens were in the process of examining him. He described them as "short **humanoids** with large, hairless heads and catlike eyes."[6] Walton managed to escape from his abductors and encountered another man who looked like a human being. The man escorted him out of the spacecraft and into a huge structure that resembled an airplane hangar. Walton passed out again, and when he woke up, he was back on Earth. He had no memory of how he had gotten back home.

A Ghostly Experience

Betty Andreasson also says she was taken aboard an alien spacecraft. She claims to have taken numerous journeys, one of which occurred on a winter evening in 1967. Andreasson was at home with her children and her parents when suddenly the lights began to flicker. Then the lights went out. The house was totally dark until the family noticed that a weird pink light was shining through the window. They watched in wide-eyed amazement as the light continued to get brighter and brighter. Without warning, everyone except Andreasson lost consciousness. She stood there in shock as four small gray aliens passed through the closed kitchen door as if they were ghosts. The leader introduced himself as Quazgaa. He explained that they had come specifically to see Andreasson.

At first she was afraid. Then she sensed that the creatures meant her no harm. They asked if she would go with them, and she agreed. She immediately began floating a few inches off the floor. Then she passed through the closed door and entered the spacecraft with the alien creatures.

First they examined Andreasson. Then they placed her in a different vessel, and she flew to another world. She described it as a place where "the atmosphere was a vibrating red color."[7] Then she was transported to a different location. This place was

Betty Andreasson, pictured undergoing hypnosis, claims that she was abducted by aliens many times.

lush with vegetation and was bathed in green light. Finally Andreasson was returned safely to her home.

Missing Time

Another encounter that ended in a safe return occurred during August of 1976. Charlie Foltz, Chuck Rak, and brothers Jack and Jim Weiner were on a camping trip in northern Maine. They were out in their canoe when they suddenly had an eerie feeling that they were being watched. When they looked behind them, they were astonished to see a large ball of bright light above the water. Because it was unlike

The Missing-Time Controversy

People who say they were abducted by aliens often refer to a block of lost time that they cannot account for. That, they believe, is evidence of their abduction. Some psychiatrists agree, but Philip Klass believes that this reasoning is nonsense, as he explains: "I experience missing time every time that I look at my watch and say: My goodness, it's two p.m., I thought it was only around noon. . . . It is automatic. It is routine."

The photographer who took this picture in 1967 claimed that the object in the sky was a UFO.

anything they had ever seen, they suspected it was a UFO. It was huge—as big as a two-story house! Its surface was covered with swirling colors that changed from red, to green, and to yellow. The men stared in amazement as the mysterious object hovered silently above the trees.

Foltz knew how to signal with a method of communication known as **Morse code**. He used his flashlight to send signals to the UFO. As though it were answering his call, it began moving closer to the canoe. The men were frightened and started paddling furiously to get back to shore. Suddenly a cone-shaped beam of light shot out of the UFO and pointed straight at them. "This is it!" thought Jack Weiner. "We'll never get away."[8]

The next thing the men knew, they were back on the shore. They watched silently as the glowing UFO flew out of sight. For a few moments they were too dazed to move or talk. Then they got up and walked back to their camp. They were shocked to see that their campfire had completely burned out.

Before the men had gone canoeing, they put huge logs on the fire so it would burn for two or three hours. They were camping deep in the woods where the nights were pitch-black. They hoped the bright flames would guide them back to their campsite. Now, as they looked at nothing but embers and ashes, the men were filled with a sense of dread. They thought they had been gone no more than half an hour. The burned-out fire, however, told them they were wrong. Several hours of their lives had disappeared, and they had no idea where the time had gone.

Buried Memories

This sort of experience is common among people who say they were abducted by aliens. Their only "evidence" of the encounter is missing time—minutes, hours, or even days that they could not account for.

Memories or Mind Tricks?

Hypnosis has long been a source of heated controversy. When people are hypnotized, it may seem as though they are recalling memories of past events. But skeptics say they may simply be thinking about their own fantasies, fears, and desires—or even remembering creatures they saw in a horror movie.

In almost all these situations, the people are confused and frightened after their experience. They remember only bits and pieces of their encounters, if anything at all. For years afterward they may suffer from nightmares and health problems without knowing why. When their memories finally come flooding back, they often feel mixed emotions: terror because of what they went through and relief that they finally know the truth.

On many occasions their memories return through **hypnosis**. People who say they had encounters with aliens often know that something happened to them. Yet they have no conscious memory of what that was. Hypnosis helps them remember hidden details.

Jim Weiner was hypnotized in 1990. For years after the canoeing incident, he had suffered from terrifying dreams about unearthly creatures. He often woke in the night feeling as though he were struggling against strange and powerful forces that he could not see. Through hypnosis he recalled what had happened to him and his friends. The beam of light from the UFO had caught them and pulled them up into the spacecraft. There they found themselves face-to-face with alien creatures. For the next few hours, the aliens communicated with them and examined them. Then they returned the men to shore.

Weiner's brother and his two friends were also hypnotized, and they told the same story. They said the aliens had not actually spoken to them in words. Instead they communicated **telepathically**, or sent messages using their minds. "They're saying things . . . with their eyes . . . in my head," Jack Weiner told the hypnotist. "They're saying, 'Don't be afraid. . . . We won't harm you. . . . Do what we say.'"[9] These were frightening memories for him to recall. But as difficult as it was for the men to relive their horrifying experience, they could finally put it behind them and move on with their lives.

Chapter 3

EARTHLY ENCOUNTERS

The experience reported by Jack Weiner and his friends was typical of many alien encounters. People often claim they saw a bright light and then found themselves in a spacecraft with alien creatures. But not all those who say they have seen aliens were transported away from this world. Some of their experiences took place on Earth.

Alien Calf-Nappers

One such incident reportedly occurred in the early 1980s in Waco, Texas. A rancher was out in his pasture searching for a missing cow. He was shocked to see two odd-looking creatures walking through his fields. They were carrying a calf between them, so he assumed they were stealing it. But they did not look anything like human thieves! The creatures were about 4 feet (1.2m) tall, with hairless heads shaped like eggs. They had no noses, and their eyes were dark and slanted, like oversize almonds. "I was afraid of them seeing me," said the rancher. "I've read all about [those] abductions and I didn't want them taking me away in some flying saucer!"[10] Fearing for his life, he forgot about the calf and ran as fast as he could to his truck.

A fanciful picture of an alien abducting cattle reflects events reported by witnesses.

Two days later the rancher returned to the place where he had seen the creatures. He found that the calf had been killed. Its skin had been stripped off and was turned inside out on the ground. Most of its bones were nowhere to be seen. He could tell that something strange had happened because there was no trace of blood. He believed that the aliens had killed the calf, even though he had no idea why.

An Eerie Prediction

New York farmer Gary Wilcox reported that he, too, had encountered aliens on his land. In April 1964, he was out tending his cows when he noticed a flash of light. Then he saw an egg-shaped object hovering near the ground. It was very large, about 20 feet (6m) long by 12 to 15 feet (3.7m to 4.5m) wide. As astonished as Wilcox was, he approached the strange vessel and tapped on it to see if it was solid. Suddenly two small alien beings dropped out of the spacecraft and landed on the ground. They were wearing silver-colored jumpsuits that covered their entire bodies. One of them began speaking to Wilcox in a deep voice. "Don't be afraid," the creature told him. "We have talked to people before."[11]

The aliens started talking to Wilcox about the future. They predicted that some bad things were going to happen in the human world. An especially disturbing message was that American and Russian astronauts were going to die in the next few years.

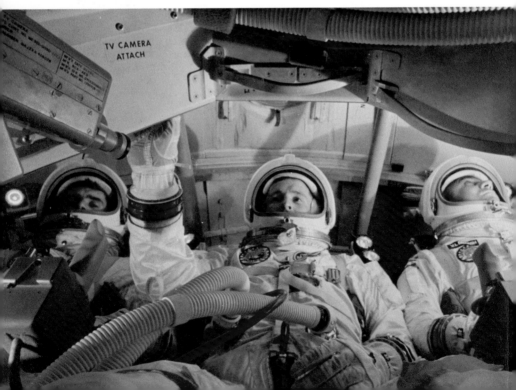

Gary Wilcox claimed the deaths of these astronauts in 1967 were predicted by an alien he encountered in 1964.

The aliens talked to Wilcox for about two hours. Then they climbed back into their spacecraft and flew away. Wilcox visited the local sheriff to report what had happened. He signed a sworn statement about what the aliens had told him.

Nine months after Wilcox's encounter, the aliens' shocking predictions came true. Three American astronauts were killed when a massive fire engulfed their space capsule. Over the next two years, two Russian astronauts (known as **cosmonauts**) had also died. One was killed when his space capsule crashed, and the other died in an airplane crash.

"He Just Stood There and Talked to Us"

Although the aliens had brought bad news to Wilcox, he had not feared them. They seemed to be peaceful creatures that did not pose any sort of threat. He believed that they just wanted to communicate with him.

Two police officers from South Carolina reported a similar experience. Officers Charles Hutchins and A.G. Huskey said they met an alien in November 1966. Although they were frightened at first, their fears vanished when they saw that the creature meant them no harm.

Hutchins and Huskey had been patrolling along an isolated road. They turned around a bend and saw a strange object hovering directly in front of

Many witnesses say that aliens are not at all frightening, despite their unusual features.

them. It was shaped like a ball, about 20 feet (6m) in diameter. They believed it was some sort of spacecraft. In the headlights of the patrol car, the object looked to be a dull gold color. Circling the bottom was a wide, flat rim.

As the spacecraft settled near the ground, the officers got out of the car and stared at it. A small door opened, and a short ladder dropped down.

Bright white light flooded the doorway, so the officers could not see inside. Then a small creature dressed in a shiny gold suit climbed down the ladder and walked toward them. It began speaking, as Hutchins explains: "We were both kind of shaky and scared. So he did most of the talking. . . . He acted like he knew exactly what he was saying and doing. . . . He just stood there and talked to us."[12] After a few minutes the creature said it was leaving and would return in two days. Then it climbed back up into the spacecraft and flew away.

Every night for the next two weeks, Hutchins and Huskey went back to the same spot to see if the little alien had returned. One evening they noticed a large orange ball sailing across the sky. But they never saw the creature again. It had not told them anything of significance, so they wondered why it had visited them.

Alien from the Stars

The opposite was true for a farmer from Switzerland named Billy Meier. He claimed that aliens he encountered had a very specific purpose in mind. They were creatures from the Pleiades, the brightest cluster of stars in the sky. After years of communicating with them telepathically, he said he met one of them face-to-face in 1975.

Meier said the aliens had told him to take his camera and go to a remote field. When he arrived, he saw a large, silver spacecraft sail over the trees and land near him. Then he watched as a beautiful, slender woman with flowing reddish gold hair left the spacecraft and walked toward him. She introduced herself as Semjase. She told Meier she was going to allow him to photograph her spacecraft. She wanted him to let humans know that they were not alone in the universe. "The Earth human calls us **extraterrestrials** or star people or whatever he wants," Semjase explained. "In truth, we are human beings like the Earth human being, but our knowledge and our wisdom and our technical capabilities are very much superior to his." As an example of her people's superior technology, Semjase pointed out her spaceship, which she called a "beamship."[13] She said it was amazingly fast. She had traveled a distance of five hundred **light-years** from the Pleiades to Earth—and she had made the journey in just seven hours!

Famous Alien Story

According to Meier, he had hundreds of meetings with Semjase over the next several years. When he told people about the visits, most of them doubted him. Some people said he was crazy. Even when Meier showed hundreds of photographs he had taken, he was accused of faking them. Yet not everyone doubted Meier's story. There were experts who said his photos could not have been faked. Other people insisted he was too honest to make up such an elaborate story.

Radio Scare

On October 30, 1938, radio programming in the United States was interrupted by news reports of the discovery of a huge flaming object. The bulletins were actually part of a radio play called *War of the Worlds*—but listeners did not know that. An actor playing a newscaster said that aliens were leaving a spacecraft and wriggling out of the shadows like gray snakes. The phony news reports seemed so real that panic broke out in many parts of the country. According to UFO skeptics, that sort of entertainment made people imagine their own alien encounters.

Although Meier's encounter was a source of criticism and doubt, it has become one of the most famous alien stories in history. Researchers have devoted untold hours to studying it, and books have been written about it. Journalist Gary Kinder spent three years studying the case. When he was finished, he admitted there were many questions that remained unanswered. "Finally I realized," he said, "that the truth of the Meier contacts will never be known."[14]

Chapter 4

ALIEN ENCOUNTERS IN THE AIR

O ther alien stories are equally as famous as Billy Meier's. Some involve people who encountered aliens not on Earth, but in the air. As with most reports of UFOs and aliens, these stories have been the subject of doubt and ridicule. Still, they are mysterious as well as unexplainable.

Vanished in the Sky!

One of the most mysterious airborne encounters reportedly occurred in October 1978. An Australian pilot named Frederick Valentich was on a training flight. He was flying a small single-engine plane, headed for King Island, Australia. Less than an hour into his flight, Valentich used his radio to contact air traffic controllers at the Melbourne airport. He said he was being "buzzed"[15] by what he thought was another aircraft. He could see four bright lights about 1,000 feet (305m) above him.

The air traffic control tower responded to Valentich, telling him that they could see nothing on their radar screens. His voice grew panicky, and he insisted that a spacecraft was getting dangerously close to his airplane. He described its shape as being long, with a metallic finish and some sort of strange green light. "It seems to be playing some sort of game," he said, ". . . flying at a speed I can't

Moments after flying over this Australian lighthouse in 1978, Frederick Valentich's plane vanished—or, some believe, was taken by aliens.

estimate. . . . It is flying past. . . . It's coming for me right now."[16]

A few moments later, Valentich told air traffic controllers that the spacecraft seemed to be directly above him. He was circling to try to get away from it, but it stayed with him. He reported that his engine was running roughly, as though it were going to stall. Then he cried, "That strange aircraft is hovering on top of me again . . . it is hovering and it's not an aircraft."[17]

The last thing the control tower heard was a strange, loud scraping noise. There was no further contact with Valentich—he had completely disappeared from the control tower's radar. No one ever saw or heard from him again. Even though the area

Bad Judgment?

When pilot Frederick Valentich had his fateful flight, he was only twenty years old. Some people speculated that his inexperience caused him to become disoriented while he was flying. If that were the case, they say, what Valentich thought was a UFO could actually have been his own lights reflected in the ocean below.

he was flying over was thoroughly searched, there was no trace of him or his airplane.

Flying Like Lightning

Thirty years before Valentich's disappearance, an even more bizarre encounter had been reported. But unlike Valentich, pilot Kenneth Arnold lived to tell about it.

The incident happened on a sunny June day in 1947, when the sky was clear and blue. Arnold, a successful businessman, pilot, and deputy federal marshal, was flying a small airplane. He had volunteered to help search for a missing aircraft that was believed to have crashed in Washington's Cascade Mountains. As he flew along at an altitude of about 9,200 feet (2.8km), a blinding flash of light caught his attention. Worrying that he had flown too close to another airplane, Arnold turned to see what caused the flash—and stared in disbelief at what he saw. Nine "peculiar looking aircraft"[18] were flying in formation close to the mountaintops. Never in his life had he seen anything like them.

Arnold noticed that the objects were traveling amazingly fast, so he decided to calculate their speed. He estimated that they were flying about 1,700 miles per hour (2,736kph)—twice the speed of sound! No aircraft of that time had ever achieved such fast speeds. Also, the objects were flying in a strange way, which Arnold later described: "[T]hey flew . . . erratically . . . like speed boats on rough water or

An artist depicts his conception of the UFO encounter described by Kenneth Arnold.

similar to the tail of a Chinese kite that I once saw bobbing in the wind . . . they fluttered and sailed, tipping their wings alternately and emitting very bright blue-white flashes from their surfaces."[19] Arnold said the objects did not whirl or spin as they flew. Rather they stayed in a fixed position.

Flying Saucers?

After Arnold landed his airplane, he told people what he had seen. He talked to other pilots and also met with a reporter from the *East Oregonian* newspaper.

Arnold described the objects by saying they flew "like saucers skipped over water."[20]

News of Arnold's strange encounter in the sky traveled fast. Before long his story appeared in newspapers all over the United States. It was also a subject of discussion on radio programs. The news media highlighted his use of the word *saucer* in their stories. Thus, the term *flying saucer* became a common term for a UFO.

Arnold had no idea that his experience would become such famous news. His only intention was to report what he saw, just as he believed any pilot

Kenneth Arnold (center) shows other pilots a photo taken of objects he saw in the sky while flying in Washington State in 1947.

should do. In a written account of the incident, he explained this: "I never asked nor wanted any [attention] for just accidentally being in the right spot at the right time to observe what I did," he wrote. "[A]nd as far as guessing what it was I observed, it is just as much a mystery to me as it is to the rest of the world."[21]

"They're on the Moon Watching Us!"

The mysterious story that Arnold reported was never solved. That is typical of stories involving encounters with UFOs and aliens. People may scoff at the accounts and develop theories about what really happened. Yet the facts will likely never be known.

The same sort of mystery surrounds the U.S. space program. More than one astronaut has claimed seeing UFOs while on space missions. One of them was the late Gordon Cooper, one of the nation's first astronauts. Throughout his career he claimed to have at least two encounters with UFOs. He described one as greenish and glowing, while the other was metallic and shaped like a disk. Cooper died believing that the U.S. government intentionally hid information about UFOs from the public.

One of the greatest mysteries of the space program involves America's first flight to the moon. The commander of the *Apollo 11* mission was astronaut Neil Armstrong. He was the first person to

Honest Mistakes

People who claim to have seen UFOs may actually have seen something unusual. But often what they saw were objects such as meteors streaking through the sky, satellites, or sunbeams. In 1981, two women in Great Britain reported seeing a large yellow blob that seemed to be wobbling and pulsating in the sky. An investigation revealed that the UFO was only the moon.

ever set foot on the moon. Armstrong has repeatedly stated that nothing unusual happened during the mission. He also insists that everything the astronauts found while visiting the moon was made public. Not everyone believes him, however. Some people are convinced that the astronauts did, in fact, discover something unusual on the moon. They could not talk about it because the National Aeronautics and Space Administration (NASA) had sworn them to secrecy.

Much of this suspicion revolves around radio transmissions from the *Apollo 11* spacecraft. Some NASA employees have claimed that the real transmission was never heard. They said it included information that NASA did not want the public to know, so the agency switched radio channels to keep it private. But according to former NASA employee Otto Binder, **ham radio** operators picked up the actual exchange between the spacecraft and mission control on Earth. In that conversation, NASA asked Armstrong what he saw, and his reply was astonishing: "These 'Babies' are huge, Sir! Enormous! . . . You wouldn't believe it! I'm telling you there are other spacecraft out there, lined up on the far side of the crater edge! They're on the Moon watching us!"[22]

The Mystery Lives On

Whether the strange *Apollo 11* transmission was genuine or faked is something only a select few people really know. That is the case with most stories of en-

NASA's mission control center listens to *Apollo 11* astronauts reporting from the moon where, some people believe, the astronauts saw UFOs in 1969.

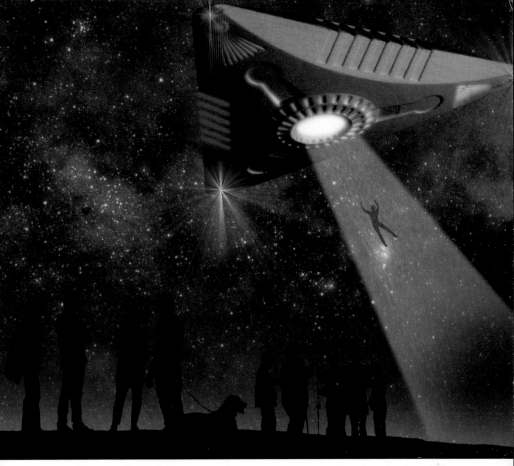

Whether people have really been abducted by aliens remains a mystery.

counters with aliens and UFOs. Are the stories real? Do alien creatures actually exist? Have people truly been abducted from Earth and whisked away in spaceships to visit distant worlds? To nonbelievers, such ideas are purely nonsense and nothing more than the product of overactive human imagination. Those who claim they have been face-to-face with alien creatures have no doubts about what they've seen. And no one will ever convince them that their experience was not real.

Notes

Chapter 1: The Unexplained

1. Quoted in "Kidnapped by UFOs?" PBS Nova Online, February 27, 1996. www.pbs.org/wgbh/nova/aliens.
2. Quoted in "Kidnapped by UFOs?"
3. Quoted by the editors of Time-Life Books in *Alien Encounters*. Alexandria, VA: Time-Life, 1992, p. 54.
4. Quoted in *Alien Encounters*, p. 56.
5. Jim Marrs, *Alien Agenda*. New York: Harper-Collins, 1997, p. x.

Chapter 2: Mysterious Journeys

6. Quoted in *Alien Encounters*, p. 9.
7. Quoted in Marrs, *Alien Agenda*, p. 214.
8. Quoted in *Alien Encounters*, p. 17.
9. Quoted in *Alien Encounters*, p. 20.

Chapter 3: Earthly Encounters

10. Quoted in Marrs, *Alien Agenda*, p. 262.
11. Quoted in John A. Keel, *The Complete Guide to Mysterious Beings*. New York: Tom Doherty, 2002, p. 166.

12. Quoted in Keel, *The Complete Guide to Mysterious Beings*, p. 170.
13. Quoted in Marrs, *Alien Agenda*, p. 203.
14. Quoted in Marrs, *Alien Agenda*, p. 203.

Chapter 4: Alien Encounters in the Air

15. Quoted in Marrs, *Alien Agenda*, p. 210.
16. Quoted in Billy Booth, "1978—Disappearance of Frederick Valentich," *UFOs/Aliens*, About.com. http://ufos.about.com/od/bestufocasefiles/p/valentich.htm.
17. Quoted in *Alien Encounters*, p. 32.
18. Kenneth Arnold, "Project 1947" (no date listed). www.project1947.com/fig/ka.htm.
19. Quoted in Marrs, *Alien Agenda*, p. 81.
20. Quoted in Jane D. Marsching, "Orbs, Blobs, and Glows: Astronauts, UFOs, and Photography," *Art Journal*, Fall 2003, p. 56.
21. Arnold, "Project 1947."
22. Quoted in Marsching, "Orbs, Blobs, and Glows: Astronauts, UFOs, and Photography," p. 56.

Glossary

abductions: Acts of being forcibly taken away.

cosmonauts: Astronauts from the former Soviet Union (present-day Russia).

extraterrestrials: Beings from a planet other than Earth.

ham radio: A type of radio that allows people to converse with each other over long distances.

humanoids: Beings that have the characteristics of humans.

hypnosis: A sleeplike state in which a person may be able to remember past events.

light-years: Measurements used for vast distances, such as between stars and the Earth.

Morse code: A system of communication that uses dots and dashes to represent letters and numbers.

telepathically: Communicated only with one's mind.

UFOs: Unidentified flying objects.

For Further Exploration

Books

Clive Gifford, *How to Meet Aliens.* New York: Franklin Watts, 2001. The first sentence of this book reads, "Have you ever looked up at the night sky and wondered, 'Are there aliens out there?'" From that point on, young readers are invited to question whether aliens exist by reading about close encounters with aliens, the search for alien life, and hoaxes.

Judith Herbst, *UFOs.* Minneapolis: Lerner, 2005. This book explores theories about whether or not UFOs really do exist. It discusses some famous UFO sightings and offers explanations about what the witnesses might actually have seen rather than UFOs. Also includes a chart that helps readers identify unusual objects in the night sky.

Jim Pike, *Tales of Horror: Aliens.* New York: Bearport, 2006. Numerous stories about alien encounters and abductions, as well as scientific explanations for eyewitness sightings. The book is enhanced with full-color photographs and drawings.

Caroline Tiger, *The UFO Hunter's Handbook*. New York: Price, Stern, Sloan, 2001. A book that explains the "paranormal," or experiences beyond what is considered normal. Includes a "UFO and alien field guide," and covers such topics as what UFOs are, what to do if one sees a UFO, and how to report such an encounter.

Periodicals

Melanie LeTourneau, "Is Anybody Out There?" *Know Your World Extra*, April 7, 2000, pp. 12–13.

Michael Morgan Pellowski, "Next Stop: Earth," *Boys' Life*, September 2003, pp. 26–29.

Web Sites

About.com "UFOs/Aliens." http://ufos.about.com. A large collection of information for anyone who is interested in aliens and UFOs. There are links to abduction stories, a UFO photo gallery, evidence of UFO crashes, and UFO groups and organizations, as well as a wide variety of other interesting items.

KidsNewsRoom www.kidsnewsroom.org. Site includes several articles about alien encounters, including one entitled "Martians!" and another called "Scientists Listen for Alien Life."

PBS Nova "Hunt for Alien Worlds." www.pbs.org/wgbh/nova/worlds. A collection of easy-to-understand facts that are known about worlds outside of Earth. Features a section called "Planet Hunt" and an essay entitled "All Alone?" that examines the possibility of life on other planets.

Index